CRACK
AND COCAINE

Designed and produced by
Aladdin Books Ltd
70 Old Compton Street
London W1

First published in the
United States in 1987 by
Gloucester Press
387 Park Avenue South
New York NY 10016

ISBN 0-531-17047-0

Printed in Belgium

Library of Congress Catalog
Card Number: 86-83110

The front cover photograph shows part of an advertisement for a concert to raise money to fight crack abuse. The back cover photograph shows a police raid on a crack house.

The author, David Browne, is a freelance writer who has reported extensively on the drug trade.

The consultant, Hugh Sykes, is a reporter for BBC Radio in London. He has reported on the drug trade in the United States and the Middle East.

Contents

CRACK
AND COCAINE

DAVID BROWNE

Illustrated by
Ron Hayward Associates

Gloucester Press
New York : Toronto : 1987

Introduction

In 1986, a new illegal drug arrived on the streets of the United States – crack, a powerful and extremely addictive form of cocaine. Within a few short months, its use had escalated to near epidemic proportions.

Deadly serious in itself, this crack explosion has also highlighted the general threat posed by the illegal drug cocaine. Cocaine abuse is a problem affecting all levels of society. Its victims include actors, sports figures, wealthy business people and ordinary workers. A high proportion of users are young. Lives have been destroyed and are continuing to be destroyed.

Although the cocaine problem is greater in the United States than anywhere else, it is by no means confined to US cities. The number of people using cocaine is rising all over the world. Cocaine traffickers are focusing on Europe as their next target. Drug officials predict that European cities could soon face an explosion of cocaine imports and the crack problem could take hold in Europe.

This book looks at the issues involved in cocaine and crack abuse. It does not concentrate in any detail on how the drugs are made or how they are taken. It is concerned with the dangers of the drugs. It also looks at the cocaine trade and at what is being done to counter the drug menace – on an individual, local and world level.

▷ The photograph shows the squalor of a "crack house" – a modern-day opium den where crack and other drugs are taken and sold. The dens are often in poor inner-city areas. To frustrate police raids, they are guarded by armed drug dealers and heavily fortified with metal doors. Since crack first appeared many thousands of these dens have opened in the United States. In New York, where this photograph was taken, police estimate there are 3,000 such dens.

4

Cocaine epidemic...

△ The increase in the use of crack and cocaine has led to an angry response from the public. People are sick of seeing their neighborhoods destroyed by the drug menace. In this photograph residents of Harlem in New York City have put toy animals and flags in the windows of a derelict building to deter drug pushers and addicts from using it. It is their way of saying: "No More Drugs."

Cocaine was once the so-called "champagne drug" used mainly by the rich and famous. It is now the fastest growing drug of abuse in the United States and is becoming a serious problem in Europe. In the last 10 years the number of people in the United States who have admitted to using the drug at least once has increased from over five million to 20 million.

The reason behind this alarming increase lies partly in the myth that cocaine is a "safe" drug which the user can control, and also because it has become relatively inexpensive.

...crack explosion

◁ Experts estimate that 5,000 people a day take cocaine for the first time. The number of users is escalating worldwide. In Italy, for example, consumption of cocaine is growing by as much as 30 per cent annually, in West Germany by 50 per cent and a similar increase is taking place in the UK.

Estimates say there could now be as many as one million people using crack in the United States and a few cases have been reported in Europe. The main reason behind the explosion in crack abuse is economics. A flood of cocaine from South America caused the price to drop considerably. Cocaine dealers then began "marketing" crack to boost their sales — they can convert cocaine into crack and sell it at a huge profit. Crack has also taken hold in such a big way because it is extremely addictive — users become dependent on the drug.

From plants to drugs

Cocaine is made from the leaves of the coca shrub that grows in the South American Andes Mountains, mainly in Bolivia and Peru. The people of the Andes who grow and harvest the coca crop chew the leaves to ward off the effects of hunger, cold and exhaustion. Farmers sell dried coca leaves to drug traders – it is by far the most profitable crop they can grow. In primitive jungle laboratories, the leaves are reduced to coca paste. This paste is then transported to more sophisticated laboratories, mainly located in Colombia, where it is further refined.

◁ Farmers openly cultivate the coca plant. Here a Peruvian peasant dries the leaves of the coca shrub at the start of the cocaine process.

▽ Every coca leaf contains roughly one per cent cocaine. The leaves are treated with chemicals to become paste, and finally powdered cocaine.

The resulting white powder is cocaine. Cocaine is a "stimulant" drug — it speeds up the body's nervous system. Users usually "snort" the drug — sniff it up the nose. A few users inject cocaine. It is also smoked in a process known as freebasing in which cocaine is burned and the vapors are inhaled. Until recently, this was an elaborate and expensive process. But then drug dealers discovered that cocaine can be reduced to its smokable form by much simpler means — by converting it to crack — and the crack phenomenon had arrived.

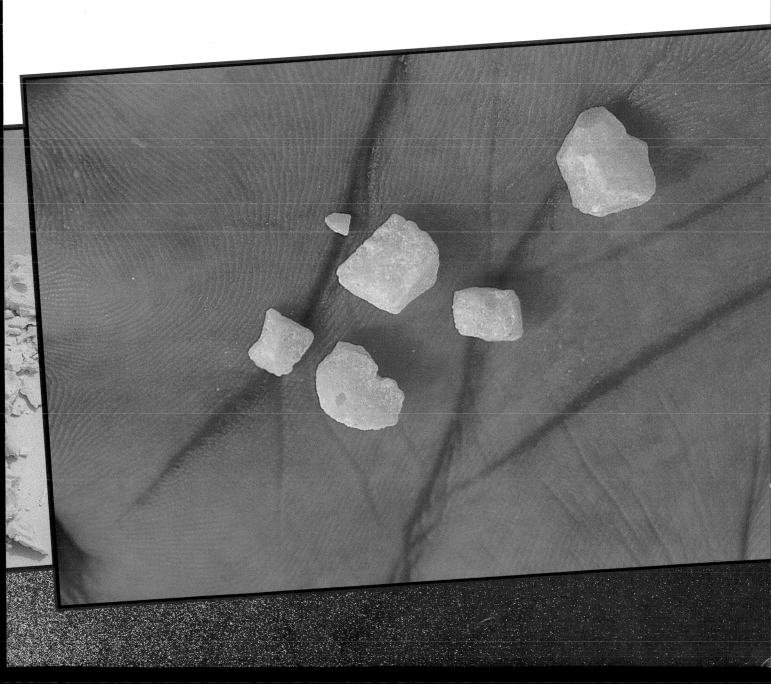

▽ Street drug dealers in the United States can buy an ounce of cocaine for $1,000-$1,500. By converting the cocaine into small crack rocks (seen here in the palm of a hand) they can make enormous profits.

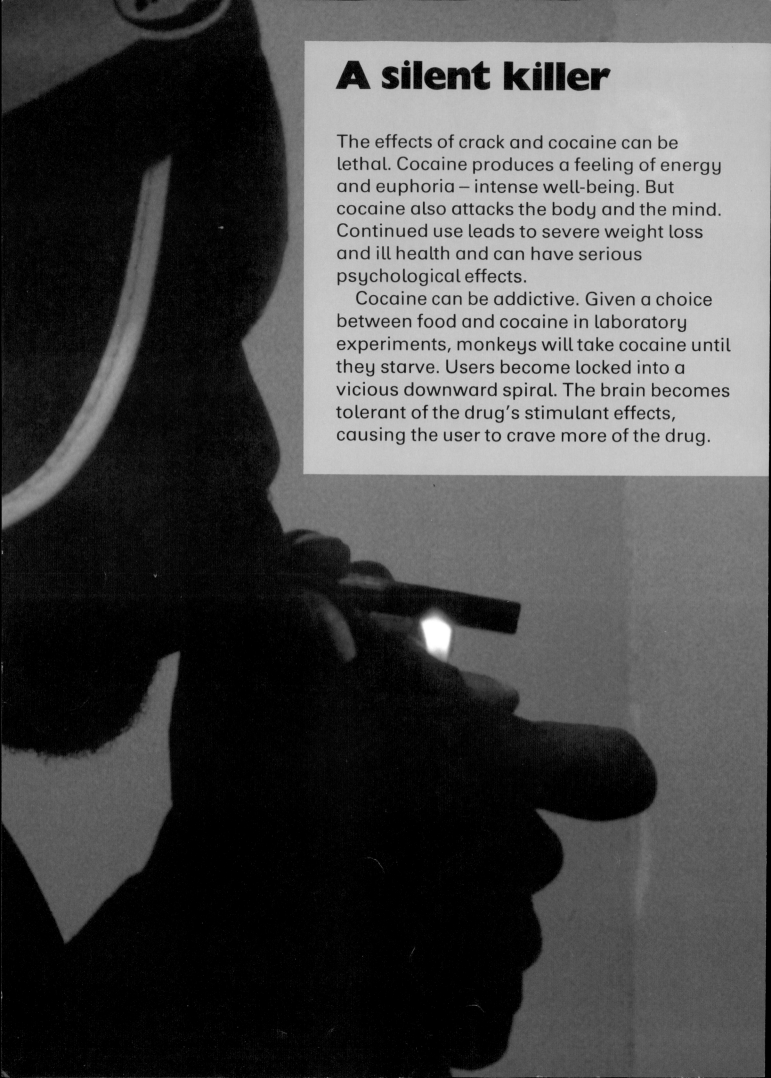

A silent killer

The effects of crack and cocaine can be lethal. Cocaine produces a feeling of energy and euphoria – intense well-being. But cocaine also attacks the body and the mind. Continued use leads to severe weight loss and ill health and can have serious psychological effects.

Cocaine can be addictive. Given a choice between food and cocaine in laboratory experiments, monkeys will take cocaine until they starve. Users become locked into a vicious downward spiral. The brain becomes tolerant of the drug's stimulant effects, causing the user to crave more of the drug.

The effects of crack can be more intense. The drug has an explosive effect on the brain as it reaches the brain faster and in greater concentrations. However, the "high" usually only lasts a few minutes and soon turns into a "crash" – the user feels very depressed.

Crack is addictive. Some experts estimate that three out of four first-time users become instantly addicted. And crack attacks the user's health with equally frightening speed.

No amount of cocaine or crack can be so small that it is safe. The drugs may not kill the first time, but the more often they are taken, the greater the chance is that they will.

Crack and cocaine have powerful psychological effects and have been known to change the personalities of users. Long-term use of crack can cause anxiety, panic attacks, difficulty in concentrating, paranoia – the feeling the user is being persecuted – and hallucinations. Life can become a nightmare of severe depression, and suicide can seem the only escape. The rate of cocaine-related deaths is increasing. In the United States, the number has tripled since 1982 – from 202 to more than 600 in 1985.

Brain: Crack euphoria can turn to depression, a desperate craving for the drug and mental health problems.

Lungs: Crack attacks the lungs and heavy use causes chest congestion. Breathing is often seriously affected.

Heart: Crack makes the heart beat dangerously fast. It can cause high blood pressure and lead to fatal heart attacks.

Skin: Crack can cause skin problems and users often have the sensation that bugs are crawling all over their bodies.

Appetite: Smoking crack suppresses hunger. This leads to weight loss and weakens the body's defense against disease.

11

Kids, coke and crack

Young people are particularly at risk from the cocaine and crack craze. Crack can be bought quite easily and cheaply in US cities. Some ruthless drug pushers actually give crack away to young people. They know that they will become addicted to the drug quickly and that this creates new customers.

However, most young people are introduced to crack and other drugs by their friends. The best response is simply to say "no," but often young people misguidedly think they have to take the drug to remain popular. This peer pressure can lead to drug dependence and often to crime. Many young crack addicts become dealers in order to finance their dependency. The only way they can afford the drug is to sell it to others. Others have turned to prostitution and theft.

▷ Children born to drug-addicted mothers are themselves addicted to the drug from birth. Mrs Clara Hale (far right) runs a clinic for drug babies in Harlem in New York City. She weans the babies off drugs and looks after them for 18 months, when they are returned to their mothers.

"Mother" Hale has saved 400 babies since she started running her clinic in 1969. In all this time she has lost only three babies, all of whom were crack babies. "I think they were born with damaged brains. They had no will to live," says Mother Hale.

High school users

The number of young people (in the 12 to 17 year-old age range) who have used cocaine has doubled in the last 10 years. The graph illustrates the increase in the number of high school seniors in the United States who are cocaine users. Latest statistics show that nearly 20 per cent of all high school seniors in the United States have used the drug at least once. As well as suffering the physical and psychological effects caused by cocaine and crack abuse, many cocaine and crack users have had to drop out of school and their education has consequently suffered.

1981   1982   1983   1984   1985

High on the job

▽ Company drug tests, like the one shown in the photograph, have some success in cutting down drug abuse by employees. But the tests are not 100 per cent reliable. Employees have to give samples of their urine for analysis to show they have not been taking drugs.

Such schemes have run into strong opposition from many people who say that they are an invasion of privacy. In 1986, in a controversial move, President Reagan proposed that this testing should be extended to include all government workers.

Many adults, deluded by the idea that cocaine is a safe drug, use it because of the energy and confidence they think it will give them at work. They see cocaine as an answer to coping with the pressures of a fast-paced society. The implications of this are serious. Workers may make mistakes if they are intoxicated by drugs.

In the UK, it is estimated that a quarter of the people with serious drug problems are workers. The cost of drug abuse to US employers – from lost productivity, absenteeism and higher accident rates – is estimated at about $33 billion by the US Government.

In an effort to cut down drug abuse in the workplace, companies all over the world are providing drug treatment programs for their employees. Some US companies have gone one step further and have compulsory drug tests.

◁ Many of the best-known victims of cocaine and crack abuse are showbusiness people. John Belushi, a leading American actor and one of the most famous comedians of his generation, died of a massive cocaine and heroin overdose in March 1982.

◁ Len Bias, aged 22, was a star of the University of Maryland basketball team. Bias was a regular user of cocaine. He died from a heart attack, which was triggered by cocaine, in July 1986.

◁ Actor Stacy Keach was arrested at Heathrow Airport, London, with a sizable quantity of cocaine. He was jailed for six months in December 1984, and his career was nearly ruined. Mr. Keach has now kicked his habit and joined the fight against crack and cocaine. He says that being a prisoner to drugs is worse than being behind bars.

A worldwide problem

The dangers posed to society by crack and cocaine have finally focused world attention on the overall dangers of drug addiction. The governments of the West have now declared open war on drugs.

The United States, where the drug problem is most acute, is leading this anti-drug crusade. Drug abuse has become a very important political and media issue. Last year the United States spent $2.1 billion on fighting drugs. This year the anti-drug budget will be increased by a further $500 million. This money will be spent on a variety of measures. For example, US Customs will recruit more officers and get more sophisticated drug-detection equipment.

▽ President and Mrs. Reagan have been at the front of the anti-drug campaign. "Drugs are a silent killer and they have the potential of tearing our country apart, just like the Civil War did," the First Lady said recently. Mrs. Reagan is particularly worried about the effect drugs are having on young people and she has lent her voice and influence to the "Just Say No" campaign, which is directed at children.

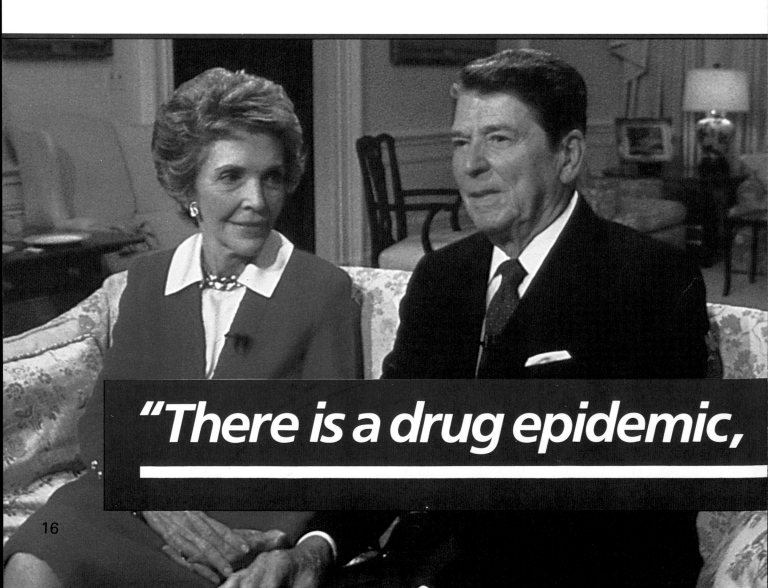

"There is a drug epidemic,

CRACK DOWN

CRO STA & SAN

PLUS SPECIAL GU
PAUL BUT
AND MANY, MA

FRIDA

ALL SEATS ARE $25.00 R
AND TICKETRON OUTLE
212/947-5850, 516/794-2

PRODUCED BY BILL GRA

THE CRACK-DOWN
a city-wide awareness and e
EDUCATION" ("ACE"). The
1) Bring role model artists fro
liaison with professional cras
City schools and drug rehabili
2) Film public service announ

YOU CAN REALLY GO PLACES WITH CRACK.

Police around the world are intensifying their action against drugs. Authorities want more arrests, more convictions and longer prison sentences. Courts in the UK and in the United States can now confiscate the property of convicted drug dealers.

Drug enforcement agencies have also taken the fight to the countries producing cocaine. The United States and Europe are providing millions of dollars to fund anti-drug programs in Peru and Bolivia. For example, farmers are being encouraged to produce alternative crops. The war is on, but it is proving a difficult war to win.

△ The dangers of crack abuse have gripped the public imagination and led to a massive media campaign. Posters warning of the dangers of drug abuse (right) are being introduced by the governments of many countries in the West.

Pop stars and other personalities have also joined the anti-crack campaign. Many perform in benefit concerts and shows, like that advertised in the photograph on the left.

and no one is safe from it."

Nancy Reagan

The South American connection

One of the major reasons for the difficulty in dealing with crack and cocaine abuse is the importance of cocaine to South America. As well as being part of the culture, cocaine has also become the economic mainstay of many countries in the area.

Peru and Bolivia grow about 90 per cent of the coca in the world. The illegal cocaine trade is worth over $1.5 billion a year to Peru, the equivalent of half their annual legal exports. In Bolivia the country and the economy would literally collapse without cocaine.

▽ Cocaine traffickers in Peru are photographed on the edge of a coca plantation. They are masked to avoid identification and heavily armed to ward off government troops and rival drug gangs.

Cocaine forms a $35 billion a year industry in South America, providing work for thousands of people. Without cocaine production many of the peasants who grow the coca would starve. Because of the huge amounts of money to be made, the drug rings are equally determined to defend the cocaine trade, with violence and bribery if necessary.

As a result, production of cocaine has led to massive corruption in these countries. Many members of the police, the army and politicians all have strong interests in the trade continuing.

◁ General Garcia Meza, ex-President of Bolivia, was deeply involved in the cocaine business. In 1980 he overthrew the government in a coup sponsored by Bolivia's cocaine barons.

△ This is a secret cocaine laboratory, deep in the South American jungle in Peru. It has just been overrun by government troops in one of their periodic drives against the drug manufacturers.

The drug barons

Carlos Lehder (pictured below), from Colombia, is one of the most notorious drug barons of recent times. He smuggled many millions of dollars' worth of cocaine from his country to Miami via the Bahamas.

Lehder bought, for cash, most of one of the islands in the Bahamas – Norman's Cay. Using armed thugs and dogs, he terrorized the remaining population to intimidate them into leaving.

Under his control, up to 30 aircraft loaded with cocaine would land on the island every night en route to Miami. Bahamian police and other officials were bribed into collaborating with this operation.

The illegal cocaine trade is run by ruthless drug barons, the "Cocaine Mafia." These men see themselves as being above the law. Murder and corruption have become a way of life. In Colombia, where their trade is worth at least $5 billion a year, they are so powerful that they murdered the Chief Justice Minister. As in this instance, the police find it very difficult to prove a case against the drug barons. They have woven protective webs around themselves by corrupting judges, customs officials and police officers.

▽ The drug barons have built up very sophisticated smuggling networks. They own fleets of aircraft and speedboats to transfer the drug from South America to the user countries. In the photograph, an airplane loaded up with cocaine takes off in Colombia.

The barons are so powerful and so rich that they are rarely, if ever, caught. They pay other people to take risks for them. They arrange for traffickers to smuggle cocaine from South America to the United States or Europe and they can make millions of dollars in profit – all without seeing a single ounce of the drug themselves.

The barons rule the traffickers and their other employees through fear. In 1985 in one incident they massacred 40 workers in Peru's Huallaga Valley because they refused to obey orders.

The cocaine barons use a variety of routes to ship cocaine from South America to the user countries. The drug may be sent through many different countries.

21

Crackdown

Because of their wealth, power and the extensive corruption surrounding the barons, fighting the drug rings is a difficult task. But policing efforts are being intensified. In the United States, the Drug Enforcement Administration has posted undercover agents in South America so that they can try to smash major cocaine networks. The American Armed Forces have also joined the fight. Recently US troops helped the Bolivian Army in a massive sweep against the cocaine trade. The soldiers blew up illegal landing strips, smashed cocaine laboratories in the jungle and burned down crops of coca.

▽ Cocaine traffickers often use dangerous and desperate methods to avoid detection. This photograph shows the stomach of a smuggler, known as a "mule." He tried to beat Customs by swallowing several small bags filled with cocaine. One of them leaked and he consequently died of a huge cocaine overdose.

International cooperation is vital to break the drug rings. Police forces around the world freely exchange information about drug trafficking and work together to stop the smugglers.

There have been some major successes. For example, in 1985 customs officers in Miami, Florida, discovered more than 1,000 kilos of cocaine, worth $600 million on the street, hidden in flower boxes on an aircraft belonging to a Colombian airline. There have been similar instances of dramatic seizures in Europe. However, the amount seized is also an indication of the enormous growth in the trade.

▽ In this photograph Miami officials discover a major cocaine shipment. Miami has become the center of the illegal cocaine trade.

As the graph illustrates, seizures of cocaine have increased dramatically in the United States in the last few years. In Europe there has been a similar increase. In the UK 7.1 kilos of cocaine were seized by the authorities in 1975; in 1985 the figure was 85.4 kilos.

Value in billions of dollars

12

9

6

3

1981   1982   1983   1984   1985

The graph shows the increase in the number of arrests for drug offenses in the United States. The years shown are 1979, '80, '81, '82, '83, '84, '85, with values ranging from 400,000 to 800,000.

A losing battle?

△ The graph shows the increase in the number of arrests for drug offenses in the United States. A similar increase is happening throughout Europe.

Crime in general is also increasing because of the crack and cocaine epidemic. One recent study in New York City showed that over half the people arrested for general criminal offenses had been using drugs, and cocaine was the drug most frequently used.

Law enforcement officials reluctantly agree they are not stemming the flood of drugs from South America. Police and Customs say they only capture about 10 per cent of all drugs smuggled. The borders of the United States are thousands of miles long — it would be impossible to police them all. It would also be impossible to check every airline passenger. Consequently, massive amounts of cocaine are still reaching the streets of the United States and Europe.

Once on the streets, the cocaine trade is no less difficult to deal with. Police worldwide are having to strengthen their forces to deal with drug offenders. The New York City police force, for example, has just created a special 300-man anti-crack squad, and in the UK the drug squad of the London police force has been increased by 50 officers to 200.

Police tactics have also been improved to try and cope with the increase in cocaine abuse. For example, in New York police conduct a "Pressure Point" campaign: a neighborhood is saturated with police. However, in the long run such measures merely push the drug trade from one area to another.

Many police officers in the United States feel they are fighting a losing battle against crack and cocaine. Arrested drug dealers are back on the streets selling drugs within days. There are not enough prison cells and not enough judges. It is true that there are more arrests, more convictions, longer sentences and more seizures of drug dealers' assets than ever before. But these statistics are more of a reflection of the volume of drug traffic, rather than an indication that the police are winning the war on cocaine.

△ Despite increased police activity, cocaine and crack are openly sold in US cities. In the photograph a crack dealer is selling the drug to a young client on a busy city street. The risk of arrest is not enough to stamp out the trade. Many street dealers only spend a few days in prison if they are caught. The prosecution system has been stretched to the breaking point and jails are already too overcrowded to admit new prisoners.

25

Finding a cure

Drug addiction is not an incurable disease. It is possible to come off crack and cocaine, and it is up to the individual to seek help.

Everybody agrees that drug addicts need help and treatment. But there is a lot of disagreement over the best way to treat addiction. The first stage in coming off drugs is called detoxification. Some clinics use other chemical drugs to help the addict come off drugs. Other clinics, which view addiction to drugs as a psychological and not a physical problem, rely on totally drug-free therapy and intensive counseling. Either course of treatment can take a very long time and often can be very expensive.

▽ Cocaine and crack addicts use the drugs as a crutch. This drug therapy course in the photograph hopes to teach people to walk again without the crutch. Addicts are encouraged to confront their addiction face-to-face in group sessions. They are asked to take a long, hard look at themselves and their lives and to find a cure through self-help and personal honesty.

Whatever type of treatment they receive, recovering addicts need follow-up care and counseling for as long as five years. Many self-help groups, like Narcotics Anonymous, have sprung up to meet this need.

Although there are many private drug abuse clinics, there are not enough treatment programs for the many addicts who cannot afford such treatment. And unfortunately, there are no firm guarantees that the programs will work. The road to drug-free living can be very long and lonely. But with determination and support from families and friends, many addicts manage to beat drug dependence.

▽ Most major cities have now set up special telephone "hot-lines" for crack and cocaine addicts who need help. This crack line in New York is manned 24 hours a day and receives literally hundreds of calls. The Cocaine National Hotline says that almost 70 per cent of all the calls it receives have to do with crack.

"Just Say No"

We know that cocaine is a dangerous drug and that crack is even more vicious, but the battle against the drugs is far from being won.

The measures taken by world governments against the drugs are meeting with only limited success. Farmers continue to grow coca crops because they are more profitable than beans or rice. Because of the massive amounts of money involved, unscrupulous people will always be found to trade in cocaine. Bribery, corruption, violence and the sheer volume of the drug trade mean that policing measures have only limited success. And as yet, on an individual level, society is not providing addicts with enough support to beat their addiction.

△ Thousands of children have signed a "Just Say No" pledge against drugs in a massive worldwide campaign.

◁ Extreme measures are not enough to stop the cocaine trade. Here, a secret airstrip and cocaine laboratories in Peru are bombed. However, local peasants welcome the raids — they are paid $10 a day by the traffickers to repair the damaged runway.

Collectively, these measures can dent the cocaine trade. But they are unlikely to have a lasting impact as long as there remains a demand for the drug. Many experts believe that warning people of the dangers of drugs is the most effective way to counter the drugs menace.

Some educators would like to see drug programs start in all schools, including kindergarten. Children would be taught about drugs just as they are taught math and English. Drug abuse is a personal issue. Nobody can force a person to take drugs. They have the right to say "NO."

Useful addresses

Where to get help

Hale House Center
68 Edgecombe Avenue
New York, NY 10031
800-235-4433
The Hale House Center is in Harlem, New York, and takes care of the children of drug addicts. Children whose parents or friends have a problem with drugs can call the toll-free number above for expert help. Hours: 9.00 am-9.00 pm Monday through Friday; 9.00 am-5.00 pm on Saturday.

National Association on Drug Abuse Problems
355 Lexington Avenue
New York, NY 10017
212-986-1170
Rehabilitation, employment and prevention programs.

National Clearinghouse for Drug Abuse Information
P.O. Box 416
Kensington, Maryland 20795
301-443-6500
You can write or call the National Clearinghouse for free information on cocaine and other drugs.

National Cocaine Hotline
800-COCAINE or 800-262-2463
This is a national toll-free number that provides callers with counseling twenty-four hours a day.

Phoenix House
164 West 74th Street
New York, NY 10023
212-595-5810
Phoenix House is a therapeutic community for all types of drug abusers.

Straight, Inc.
P.O. Box 21686
St. Petersburg, Florida 33742
813-576-8928
Straight's objective is to treat drug-using adolescents through the use of an intensive, highly structured, progressive therapeutic process. Straight works to retrain adolescents in the values and rules of their culture and helps them to unlearn the rules and behavior of the drug subculture. The program takes six to eighteen months, and has centers in Atlanta, GA; Cincinnati, OH; and Washington, DC.

Chronology

1885 Cocaine is viewed as the wonder drug of the era, a harmless cure-all.

1903 Experts begin to recognize the dangers of cocaine addiction, and cocaine is removed from Coca-Cola.

1906 The United States tightens up controls against cocaine through the Pure Food and Drug Act.

1914 Cocaine is effectively banned in the United States by the Harrison Narcotic Act.

1916 Cocaine is banned in the UK.

1960s Cocaine becomes a drug favored by the rich and the jet set.

1970s Cocaine from South America begins to flood the market in the United States and Europe.

1982 The Bahamas begins to report a major problem with crack addiction.

1984-86 Crack spreads to New York. The first cases of addiction are reported in December 1984.

1986 The US government says the country is suffering from a cocaine epidemic. Drug abuse becomes an election and media issue. The West declares open war on drugs.

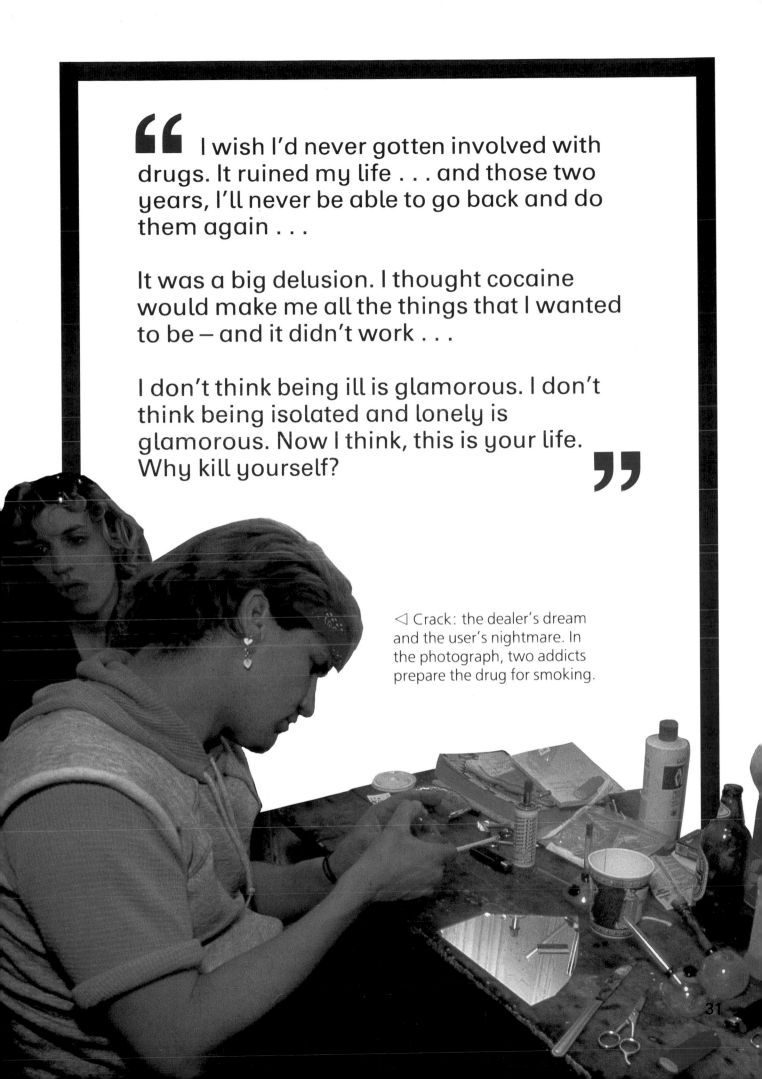

" I wish I'd never gotten involved with drugs. It ruined my life . . . and those two years, I'll never be able to go back and do them again . . .

It was a big delusion. I thought cocaine would make me all the things that I wanted to be – and it didn't work . . .

I don't think being ill is glamorous. I don't think being isolated and lonely is glamorous. Now I think, this is your life. Why kill yourself? **"**

◁ Crack: the dealer's dream and the user's nightmare. In the photograph, two addicts prepare the drug for smoking.

31

Index

Photographic Credits:
Cover and pages 4/5, 13, 17, 25 and 27: David Browne; pages 6/7, 10/11, 14, 28 and back cover: Colorific; pages 8, 9, 15, 18/19, 19, 20/21, 23, 24, 28/29 and 31: Frank Spooner; page 8: Hutchinson Library; pages 12/13: Janine Weidel Photography; pages 15 and 19: Popperfoto; page 15: Associated Press; page 16: Rex Features; page 17: Newsday; pages 20 and 22: David West; page 26: Network.

PRINTED IN BELGIUM BY
proost
INTERNATIONAL BOOK PRODUCTION

j363.293 Browne, David.
BRO
       Crack and cocaine

$11.90   f

DATE			
JAN 8			
OCT 26			
JAN 9			
OCT 26			
FEB 1 2 2002			
JAN 1 6 2015			